932
DAV

David, Rosalie

Ancient Egypt

DATE DUE

FEB 7 1991			

HISTORY AS EVIDENCE
ANCIENT
EGYPT

ROSALIE AND ANTONY E. DAVID
Illustrated by David Salariya and Shirley Willis

Warwick Press

Contents

Editor: Caroline Royds
Designer: Ben White

The publishers wish to thank the following for supplying
photographs for this book: 8 top and bottom British Museum;
10 top Crown Copyright Reserved, Institute of Archaeology,
London University; 14 top R. David, bottom A. R. David;
15 bottom ZEFA; 16–17 top Michael Holford; 17 bottom
Manchester Museum; 19 bottom A. A. M. van der Heyden;
20 left Manchester Museum; 22 R. David; 28–29 top Courtesy
Museum of Fine Arts, Boston; 30 top Roger Wood; 32 bottom
Michael Holford.

Published 1984 by Warwick Press,
387 Park Avenue South, New York, New York 10016.

First published in Great Britain by
Kingfisher Books Limited 1984.

Printed in Italy by Vallardi Industrie Grafiche, Milan.

Library of Congress Catalog Card No. 84-50695

ISBN 0-531-03744-4

Introduction

Egypt had one of the earliest and most spectacular of the world's civilizations. As the map clearly shows, the country was hemmed in by natural barriers – the desert to the west, the Mediterranean to the north, the Red Sea on the east, and the regions of tropical Africa to the south. These protected it for many generations from foreign invasion and other cultural influences, which meant that a unique and distinctive civilization was able to develop.

The dryness and warmth of the Egyptian climate has ensured that many of the monuments and artefacts of this ancient civilization have been preserved. Visitors to the country can still see pyramids, temples and tombs, and there are large collections of Egyptian antiquities in museums around the world. The religious and funerary beliefs of the ancient Egyptians were centered around the need to preserve the bodies of the dead and to equip their tombs with a wide range of goods. These all supply Egyptologists with a wealth of information. The decipherment of texts, written in hieroglyphs and the related scripts of Hieratic and Demotic, provide further insight into their thoughts and beliefs.

One of the written pieces of evidence we have is a history of Egypt – the work of a priest called Manetho. In it he divides a list of kings into "dynasties." A dynasty usually includes rulers of one family; one is sometimes connected to its successor by family links, or a new dynasty can be introduced by a king who has seized the throne. The Egyptian dynasties are arranged together under general headings: Predynastic period (c.5000–c.3100 BC); Archaic Period (Dynasties 1 and 2, 3100–2686 BC); Old Kingdom (Dynasties 3–6, 2686–2181 BC); First Intermediate Period (Dynasties 7–11, 2181–1991 BC); Middle Kingdom (Dynasty 12, 1991–1786 BC); Second Intermediate Period (Dynasties 13–17, 1786–1552 BC); New Kingdom (Dynasties 18–20, 1552–1069 BC); Third Intermediate Period (Dynasties 21–26, 1069–525 BC); Late Period (Dynasties 27–31, 525–332 BC); Graeco-Roman Period (332 BC–AD 641). The great eras of Egyptian history were the Old, Middle and New Kingdoms.

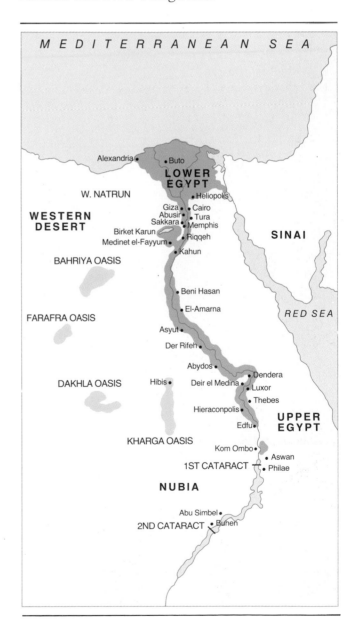

The King

The history of Egypt goes back about 5000 years. It became a kingdom when the north and south were united by King Menes after he conquered the north in 3100 BC. The Egyptians called the north Lower Egypt, the south Upper Egypt and the whole country 'Kemet.'

The society of ancient Egypt can be seen as a pyramid. At the top was the king, who was believed to be the chief god's son and to have godlike powers. He often married his own sister to inherit the throne; their son would become the next ruler and marry his sister. The king was head of the army, the navy, the law courts and the state religion. He could approach the gods on behalf of the people, and he owned all the land, property, and even people in Egypt.

Below the king were the nobles, who were sometimes members of his own family. They owned land and property, subject to his favor, and held top posts in the government. On occasions, they became a threat and the king had to limit their power. Next came the minor state officials responsible for all the daily business of government – running the Treasury, the Civil Service and the Records Office. The next level was made up of craftsmen – all the stonemasons, carpenters, jewelers and smiths employed on the building, decorating and equipping of the king's tomb. At the bottom of the pyramid were the ordinary workers who grew the food and worked on the royal buildings.

Above: The gold mask found over the mummy of the boy-king Tutankhamun. His tomb was discovered at Thebes in Upper Egypt. It was cut into the rock in the Valley of the Kings. The mummy was encased in three gold coffins as well as this mask. A complete set of funerary jewelry was found between the layers of mummy bandages.

Left: Part of an ostrich feather fan. It shows the king in a chariot returning from an ostrich hunt. This is one of the treasures from Tutankhamun's tomb, now in the Cairo Museum. Ostrich hunting was probably a favorite pastime of this king, who was only about nineteen when he died, having ruled Egypt for some ten years. When Howard Carter and his patron, Lord Carnarvon, discovered this tomb in 1922, it caused worldwide interest, because it was the only royal tomb to have been found in the Valley of the Kings which had not been heavily plundered by tomb robbers. Many of the objects from the tomb tell us something of Tutankhamun's life and interests.

Although Egypt became a great state and the king had many duties to perform, he still led his army, offered gifts to gods in the main temple, and listened to some of the pleas about legal cases from his subjects, even if they were very poor. Audiences with the king would be held in the reception hall of the palace, where his courtiers and servants gathered, moving fans to make a breeze.

Palaces, temples and tombs were all built on the same plan; and ordinary houses also had the same main areas – an approach, a reception hall or room and a bedroom or a sanctuary. There were other rooms for the preparation of food and for storing clothes and possessions. As a house or palace was the home of a living person, so temples and tombs were the "houses" of the gods and the dead, who were thought to need the same things as the living – clothes, food and drink, games and enjoyment, and a place for rest. While many of the tombs and temples, being built of stone, have survived, most of the mud-brick palaces and houses are lost. However, we know that they had wall-scenes painted with bright colors, and columns to support the roof. All the palaces had fine furniture, often overlaid with gold.

Below: The great hall of King Tutankhamun's palace. Unlike the temples or tombs which were made of stone, houses and even palaces were of mud-brick. There were areas for living in these palaces, but a large part would be used for the king's official administrative duties. Although a god-king, courtiers would advise him on state matters.

A Royal Funeral

In the Old Kingdom, when Egyptian civilization produced many major new ideas, it became the custom to bury kings in special tombs which we call "pyramids." Built at the edge of the desert, these huge constructions were joined to the Nile by a long causeway and furnished with a series of chambers for the king's use during his eternal life. This scene reconstructs the arrival of King Sahure's funeral procession at the pyramid at Abusir in around 2473 BC. Boats bring the body and its attendants along the river to the pyramid, with the king's coffins and the goods – clothing, furniture, food and possessions – which are to be buried with him. After landing, the procession will enter the Valley Building, where the body may have been mummified and the religious rituals performed. It will then pass up the Causeway to the Mortuary Temple for the funeral rites, before the body is taken into the pyramid and buried. Priests will say magical spells for the king to join the sun-god Re in the sky. The remains of wooden boats found buried outside some pyramids suggest that they were for the king to use to sail around the sky.

Above: The remains of King Sahure's pyramid at Abusir. In the time of the Old Kingdom pyramids were built at many sites, including Saqqara and Giza. The most famous is the Great Pyramid at Giza. Sahure's pyramid, which was built later, is more ruined.

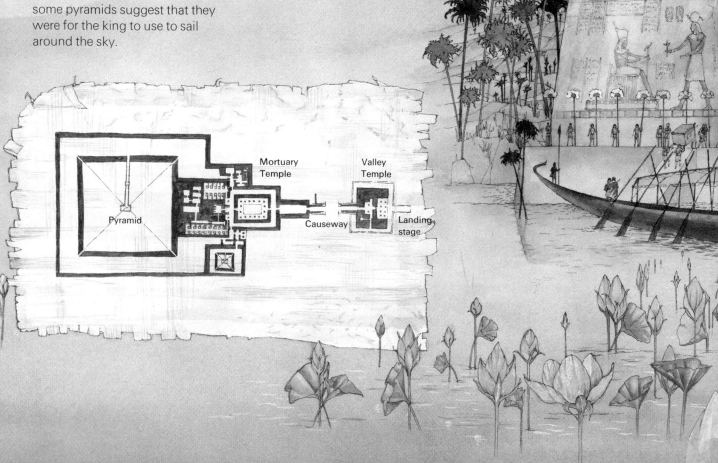

Pyramid

Mortuary Temple

Valley Temple

Causeway

Landing stage

Building a Pyramid

"A ramp to the sky is built for him, that he may go up to the sky on it . . .
He flies as a bird, and he settles as a beetle on an empty seat that is in the
ship of Re."

Some of the pyramids were decorated inside with spells carved on the walls. These are known as the "Pyramid Texts." They were magical spells, like the one above, which were repeated with the idea that magic could move the king's body to the sky. The "ramp" mentioned in the spell probably referred to the pyramid itself. Most pyramids have been explored by archaeologists, but apart from the large stone coffin (sarcophagus) in which the body was buried, few remains have been found either of the bodies or of the treasures which were buried with the kings. In many cases, the pyramid was probably robbed soon after the king's burial. One of the reasons why the Egyptians stopped building pyramids was because they could be so easily seen and plundered. It is possible, however, that undiscovered chambers remain in some of the pyramids, and that archaeologists may still make new finds.

In the last century, the famous British Egyptologist, Sir W. Flinders Petrie, discovered wonderful jewelry belonging to royal princesses in tombs near the pyramid of King Sesostris II at Lahun. Some queens seem to have had separate tombs, but the small pyramids which we see at Giza may also have been used for them, unless these housed the king's own internal organs which were removed at the time of mummification. Since no human remains have been found there, their use remains uncertain.

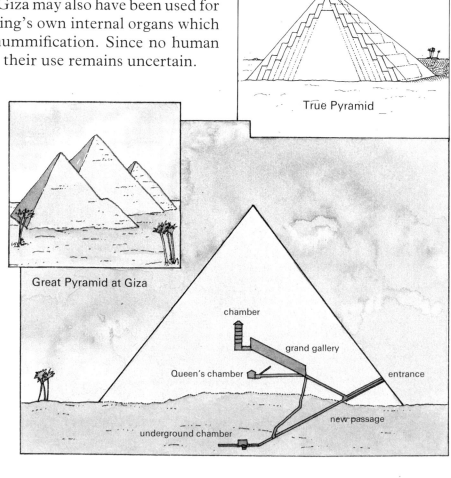

Step Pyramid

Bent Pyramid

True Pyramid

Above and right: Diagrams showing the development of the pyramid, and the Great Pyramid at Giza. The first pyramid, built close to the capital, Memphis, had steps. The site, called Saqqara today, was the burial place of King Zoser. The man who built it, Imhotep, may have intended to build a series of tombs one on top of another; each step looks like the outline of the early tombs which Egyptologists call "mastabas" ("mastaba" means "bench-shaped" in Arabic). The Egyptians moved from building step pyramids to true pyramids, going through various stages in between. One of these was the "bent" pyramid where changes were made to the angles of the sides; the location of the burial area might be inside or below ground.

Great Pyramid at Giza

chamber

grand gallery

Queen's chamber

entrance

new passage

underground chamber

12

The Egyptians have left no written account of how they built the pyramids. We have to look at these buildings, and the few tools which have been found, to try to understand their building methods. There were architects, skilled craftsmen and overseers, but the workforce for the heavy laboring was supplied by the peasants. Because the Nile river flooded the countryside for three months of every year, it became impossible during that time to work the land, so the peasants would move to the site and help to build the pyramid.

Although some of the stone was quarried locally, granite (a very hard stone) was brought by river from Aswan, over 500 miles to the south, and then dragged on rollers from the river to the pyramid site. Ramps were built to allow the men to drag the stones up to the work level. First the core was built, and then the limestone facing was put on, working from the top down to the ground. The ramps would be removed as they worked downward. Simple tools of bronze and stone were used, but few of these have been found. A large workforce and craftsmen with special skills enabled the Egyptians to build these great tombs.

Below: Pyramid builders at work. Nile boats are arriving with their cargoes of stone, while the masons are rough-cutting the stones which will be smoothed and finished when they are in position. Other gangs of men drag the great stones up the ramp on wooden rollers to the work level. The workers probably lived in temporary huts near the site; and mud-brick villages were built for them and their families in the area. They were paid in food – bread, onions and beer. The men were probably willing workers because they believed that helping to build the king's pyramid gave them a chance to share in his life after death.

Religion

The Egyptians worshiped many different gods. As well as state gods and local gods, who both had temples and priests, there were household gods prayed to by ordinary people at home. Many gods had half-human and half-animal or bird form.

The Egyptians were very religious people. We can learn a great deal about their beliefs from their writings, their buildings and religious furnishings. Temples and tombs, which have survived because they were built of stone, are decorated with wall-scenes showing the religious services which went on in the temples and the Egyptian view of life after death. Small statues of the household gods have also been discovered which tell us something of the part religion played in the day-to-day life of ordinary families. The favorite of these was Bes (seen in the photograph on the right). He was a jolly dwarf, who was god of music and dancing. The temple gods were more important and received daily food from the priests. Most priests spent only three months of every year in the temple; for the rest of the time they were doctors, lawyers or scribes, living at home with their families. The gods of the Egyptians played many different parts – some were gods of Nature, of the sun, moon, sky and earth; others were gods of arts and crafts, and healing; while many were members of family groups.

Below: A temple wall carved with scenes of the king making offerings to the gods. The king is always shown looking after the gods, although these duties would normally have been carried out by the high-priest of each temple.

Above: The god's sanctuary. The temples were very dark and the sanctuary was always at the back of the temple, so the priests would have carried flares. They wore white linen clothes and sandals, and their heads were shaven.

Below: An outside view of the temple at Abu Simbel (see above).

The temple was the god's house; the priests his servants. In every temple in Egypt, every day, the priests would look after the god's needs. In the morning, they would go to the sanctuary, take the statue from its shrine and remove the clothing and makeup from the previous day. They would clean the statue by burning incense, then dress it in fresh clothes, put on new makeup and present it with jewelry and crowns. Finally a meal was placed in front of it. This would remain untouched till it was removed and eaten by the priests as payment for their duties. At midday, another meal was presented, and in the evening the priests would bring a final meal before the statue was put back in the shrine for its night rest. Women were not allowed to become priests, but they did perform as singers and dancers in the temples. They sang to wake the god up every morning, during a service called the "Daily Temple Ritual."

The gods also needed amusement and entertainment, and several times a year festivals were held. These were not the same in every temple, but in some the god left his temple and visited his wife in her temple which would be some miles away. Ordinary people often traveled many miles to take part in these festivals, and there would be a lot of singing and dancing as the god's statue was carried in a wooden boat from the temple to the river for its journey, accompanied by the priests.

Tombs

Although kings were buried in pyramids in the earlier part of Egypt's history, the noblemen and their families were always buried in tombs. These were sometimes "mastaba-tombs," with an area below ground for the burial and a bench-shaped construction above ground which marked the tomb. Sometimes they were cut into the cliffs, with a burial pit and a chamber or pillared court where the family could visit. All the tombs were regarded as "houses" for the dead to live in.

Although in the Old Kingdom only the king was thought to have a real afterlife, from the Middle Kingdom onward all people, rich or poor, were believed to go on living after death. This accounts for the great popularity of Osiris, the god of vegetation and the underworld, King of the Dead, who promised all his followers eternal life. To some extent, people had different ideas of where this afterlife would be spent according to their wealth and status. The king would travel with the gods in the sky, the very poor would continue to tend the land – in the "Fields of Reeds" in Osiris' kingdom – but the wealthy hoped to spend time in their tomb, their "House of Eternity." By placing scenes on the walls which depicted many of their favorite occupations and pastimes in life, and by putting into the tomb their possessions and models of servants – brewers, bakers and cooks – to provide a supply of food in the next world, they hoped, by means of magic, to recreate a pleasant existence.

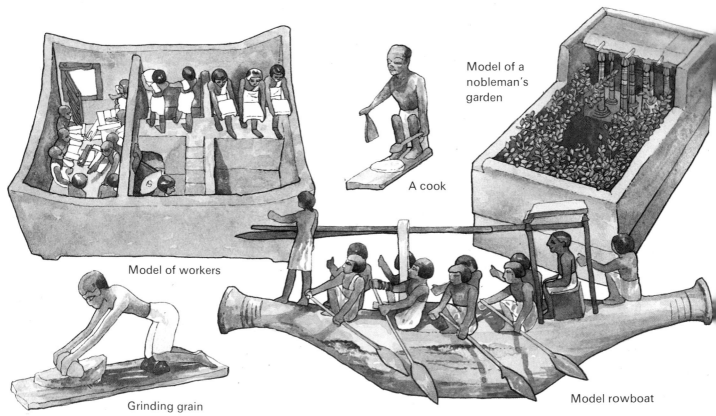

Model of a nobleman's garden

A cook

Model of workers

Grinding grain

Model rowboat

Food and drink were essential provisions for the afterlife. At first the family had brought offerings of food to the tomb but, over several generations, this involved visiting too many graves. Special priests were then employed to do this, but after some time, they too neglected their duties. Finally, the Egyptians provided a menu painted on the tomb wall, and models of food and of servants making food which, they believed, could be made to exist by magic. The family still continued to bring offerings of food to a special chapel to ensure that the dead person had a constant supply of food.

The tombs, crammed with furniture, clothing, jewelry and the other possessions for eternity, inevitably attracted tomb-robbers. While excavating the tomb of a rich man at Riqqeh in central Egypt, archaeologists discovered dramatic evidence of this. They found the mummy of the owner with a rare and beautiful piece of jewelry called a pectoral hung around its neck. Across the mummy lay the body of a long-dead tomb-robber. He had been about to snatch the pectoral when part of the tomb collapsed and he was killed. This was a particularly fascinating find, as you can see from the reconstruction below. However, all the tombs with their painted scenes and, where they still remain, the tomb possessions, provide Egyptologists with a great deal of information about funerary and burial customs, and about the daily lives of the people.

Above: A wall scene from a tomb depicting the nobleman Nebamun hunting in the marshes.
Below: The Riqqeh Pectoral, now in the Manchester Museum.

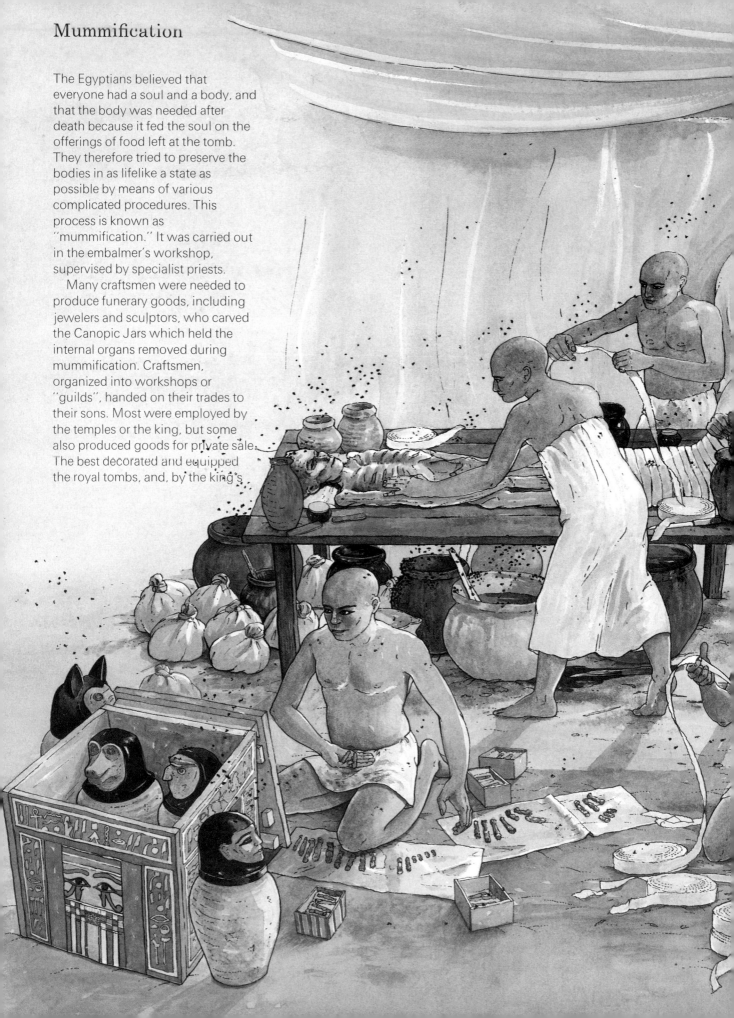

Mummification

The Egyptians believed that everyone had a soul and a body, and that the body was needed after death because it fed the soul on the offerings of food left at the tomb. They therefore tried to preserve the bodies in as lifelike a state as possible by means of various complicated procedures. This process is known as "mummification." It was carried out in the embalmer's workshop, supervised by specialist priests.

Many craftsmen were needed to produce funerary goods, including jewelers and sculptors, who carved the Canopic Jars which held the internal organs removed during mummification. Craftsmen, organized into workshops or "guilds", handed on their trades to their sons. Most were employed by the temples or the king, but some also produced goods for private sale. The best decorated and equipped the royal tombs, and, by the king's favor, could be seconded to prepare the tombs of noblemen and officials. An important group were the coffin-makers. Coffins were used before mummification was introduced. Simple, woven basketwork coffins held bodies buried in shallow graves or mastaba tombs. Then pottery coffins came into fashion, but neither protected the body satisfactorily. Pottery coffins broke and basketwork collapsed and decayed. Nevertheless, even after mummification was developed, these continued to be used, especially for the lower classes who were not mummified. As the tombs became more elaborate and were owned by more people, fine rectangular stone and wood coffins were introduced. Stylized body coffins, carved to represent a mummy, also appeared. These sometimes contained cartonnage cases. Religious scenes and texts, believed to help the dead in the afterlife, decorated these coffins. The owner's name and profession were now written on the coffin.

Below, a priest supervises a stage of mummification. He wears the jackal mask of Anubis, god of cemeteries and mummification.

Canopic jars

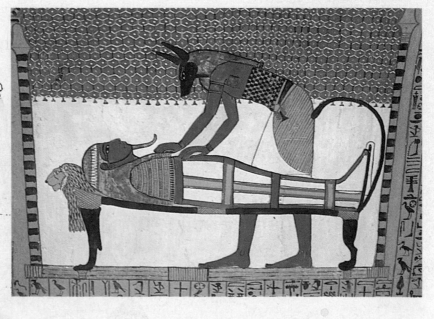

Mummies and Medicine

By about 2700 BC, the Egyptians had developed the process of mummification. In earliest times they buried the dead in simple pits in the sand. The area of cultivatable land in Egypt was very small, and too valuable to be used for burial, so the cemeteries were placed at the edge of the desert. The bodies, in direct contact with the sand, remained in a preserved state because they dried out before they had time to decay and become skeletons. Sometimes the wind would blow the sand away from the graves and expose these preserved bodies, so the living became aware that bodies could be preserved and thought that this meant that the dead needed them after death.

When the Egyptians started building the more elaborate mastaba tombs with brick-lined burial pits, the bodies began to decay rapidly because they were no longer directly in contact with the drying agent. Over many years, therefore, various attempts were made to make the body look lifelike so that the soul could recognize and use it after death. Bandages soaked in a gummy substance were molded around it and features painted on the outer wrappings. But soon after the first pyramids were built, the Egyptians developed a chemical method for drying and preserving the body which we call mummification. The word comes from the Arabic word "mummia," which means bitumen. Some of the later mummies have a blackened appearance as if they were covered in bitumen, so this name was wrongly applied to them and has survived.

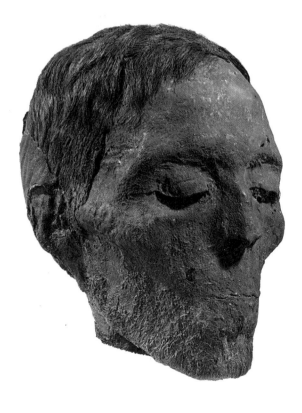

Left: A mummified head of the Ptolemaic period (c. 100 BC). Many Greeks lived in Egypt then, and adopted Egyptian funerary customs, including mummification. Usually, the mummies are less well-preserved but the outer bandages and cases are very elaborate. However, this head is intact, and you can see the remains of hair and a sparse beard. Experiments have shown that the quality of mummification was partly dependent upon the number of times the natron (the dehydrating agent) was re-used.

Above: Today the carefully wrappe mummies can be examined by specialists using various technique such as radiology, serology, electro microscopy and histology. In Manchester, England, in 1975 a team of experts carried out the first unwrapping of a mummy for over 70 years. Using new, non-

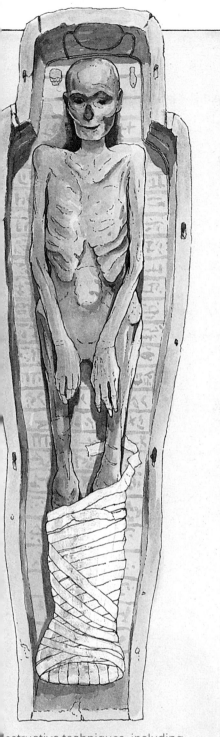

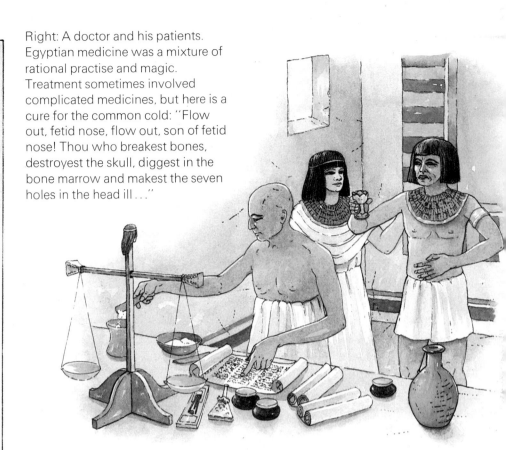

Right: A doctor and his patients. Egyptian medicine was a mixture of rational practise and magic. Treatment sometimes involved complicated medicines, but here is a cure for the common cold: "Flow out, fetid nose, flow out, son of fetid nose! Thou who breakest bones, destroyest the skull, diggest in the bone marrow and makest the seven holes in the head ill..."

estructive techniques, including
ndoscopy, they were able to
atalog information about illness
nd disease in ancient Egypt which
vas then stored on a computer.
ventually we may be able to see
atterns of disease prevailing at
ifferent periods.

The only written accounts of mummification survive in the work of the Greek historians Herodotus and Diodorus Siculus. But the physical evidence of the mummies themselves helps us to understand the process. Over seventy days (thirty of which were probably taken up with religious rites), the most expensive process involved the removal of the viscera (internal organs) through a cut in the stomach. Then both the body and the viscera were treated with dry natron (a salt compound) to remove the fluids from the tissues. The organs were sometimes wrapped and replaced in the body or put in Canopic jars, the stoppers of which were often carved to represent the four demi-gods who protected them. The body, dried and treated with spices, was wrapped in layers of bandages, between which were inserted jewelry and amulets to bring magical protection.

Even animals, believed to represent certain gods, were mummified in large numbers, especially in the later periods. At first, only the king and his family were mummified, but this was gradually extended, until, in the last years, anyone who could afford it was mummified. The poorest people were still buried simply in the sand. The process of mummification made the Egyptians aware of the anatomy of the body, and this knowledge helped them to develop the earliest medical system, which has in part come down to us from the Greeks and Romans, through medieval Europe.

Daily Life

Most Egyptian finds come from the tombs. Very few town sites have been discovered because towns and villages were built of mud-brick, and as buildings fell down, others were erected on top of them. The discovery of a workmen's town of about 1900 BC was therefore an important addition to our knowledge.

In the 1890s, the famous Egyptologist, Flinders Petrie, discovered and excavated the town of Kahun. He wrote in his diary: "Who could have ventured to hope for a complete, untouched and unencumbered town of the 12th Dynasty? It is a prize beyond all probability". Kahun was built to house the families of the workmen and officials engaged in the construction and maintenance of the pyramid and temple of King Sesostris II at Lahun in the Fayoum Oasis. It dates to the Middle Kingdom (about 1900 BC) and continued to be occupied for many years after the king's reign. However, the town had eventually been deserted for some reason, and Petrie's excavations revealed not only rows of houses – some terraces for the workmen and other larger houses for officials – but also all the everyday objects left behind.

Other workmen's towns were later discovered – at Deir el Medina near Thebes, where the workmen engaged on the royal tombs were housed, and at El Amarna. Presumably every major royal building project had a similar town to house its workforce. Kahun is the earliest so far found, and it contained an abundance of objects and documents which gave details of the medical, veterinary and legal practices of the community.

Above: An ancient Egyptian using a fire-stick. Since only selected items were placed in the tombs, many ordinary articles were unknown till the discoveries at Kahun. It was not known, for example, how the Egyptians made fire until several fire-sticks were found there. The fire-stick works on the bow-drill principle. A capstone of hard stone is pressed down on a wooden stick, one end of which is placed in a hole in the matrix. The bow-drill, held in the other hand, is moved rapidly and the friction causes sparks to be kindled at the matrix. Very dry twigs and leaves would be used to kindle fire from these sparks.

Right: The remains of the pyramid at Lahun today. Nearby, covered now by sand after Petrie's excavations, is the town of Kahun. Unlike the other cities and towns of Egypt, which grew randomly, the workmen's towns were laid out by a single architect to a fixed plan. There is little evidence of later building, as such towns were only used while the site was important as the royal burial place. Such towns, surrounded by a thick enclosure wall and situated in an isolated area near the royal tomb, were kept separate because their inhabitants knew the secret of the position and structure of the tomb.

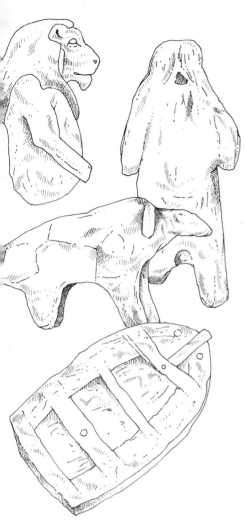

This unique collection of finds is now in museums around the world. Petrie's excavation was financially supported by a number of patrons, but one of the major contributors was a textile manufacturer, Jesse Haworth. Because of his generosity, Haworth received a major share of the finds from the site, which he later left to the Manchester Museum. Most of the other discoveries are at the Petrie Museum at University College, London. Some years ago, it was decided to examine some of the material from Kahun using modern scientific techniques, to try and answer certain questions about the site and the technology of the tools found there.

Using the facilities of the Manchester University reactor, metals from the site were investigated, and a study of the possible sources of the clay used in the pottery begun. The technique, called Neutron Activation Analysis, can help to identify how much of the pottery at Kahun originated outside Egypt. This technique involves taking samples from the object, irradiating them in the reactor, and obtaining a breakdown of their various elements. This can then be compared with the known composition of natural materials from Egypt and elsewhere. It can then be seen if the objects are of local or foreign manufacture. The outcome of this investigation will hopefully throw some light on Petrie's claim that a large proportion of the workforce living there was from another area of the ancient world.

Above: Clay toys representing a lion, a man, a pig and a boat, found at Kahun. There seems to have been a minor toy-making industry in the town (in one house a supply of hair was discovered, ready for insertion into wooden dolls), but some toys were made by children. Balls, whip tops and tip cats were also found.

Right: A reconstruction of a kitchen at Kahun based on material found during excavation. This included pots, household brushes, grindstones, and a strange pottery container which may have been used to rear chickens or as a portable oven. Builders' tools were also uncovered, including plasterers' floats and mud-brick molds of a kind still used today. One plasterer's float still had remains of mud sticking to it where the plasterer forgot to clean it some 4000 years ago.

Kahun, a working town

Kahun was built in a slight depression surrounded by cliffs. This location made it easy to isolate the population. The houses were built of mud-brick and some had vaulted brick roofs. Petrie cleared some 2000 chambers and found evidence

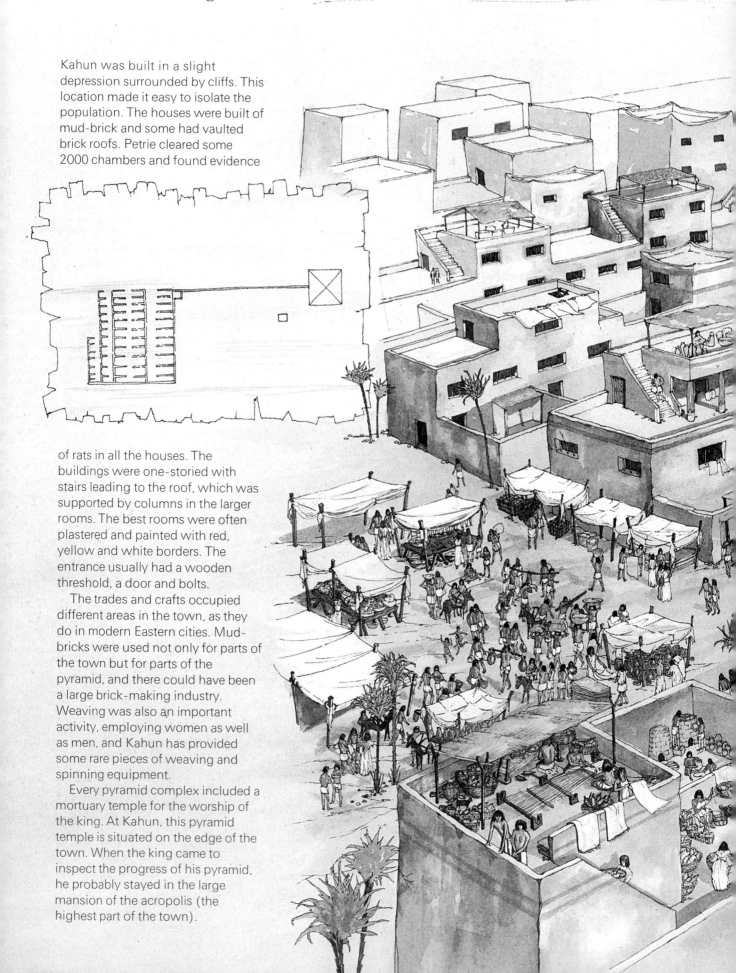

of rats in all the houses. The buildings were one-storied with stairs leading to the roof, which was supported by columns in the larger rooms. The best rooms were often plastered and painted with red, yellow and white borders. The entrance usually had a wooden threshold, a door and bolts.

The trades and crafts occupied different areas in the town, as they do in modern Eastern cities. Mud-bricks were used not only for parts of the town but for parts of the pyramid, and there could have been a large brick-making industry. Weaving was also an important activity, employing women as well as men, and Kahun has provided some rare pieces of weaving and spinning equipment.

Every pyramid complex included a mortuary temple for the worship of the king. At Kahun, this pyramid temple is situated on the edge of the town. When the king came to inspect the progress of his pyramid, he probably stayed in the large mansion of the acropolis (the highest part of the town).

Agriculture

Herodotus called Egypt the "gift of the Nile." The country has very little rainfall, so crop-growing is dependent on the Nile floods. These are the result of the heavy rains of tropical regions far to the south. Before this century, when dams were built along the river, the floods varied greatly in size – one year could bring drought, another too much water. Now the dams hold back the water and allow it through when required. Every year before this, the rising of the waters was first seen at Aswan at the end of June, reaching its full height at Cairo towards the end of September, and sinking to its lowest level in April. From earliest times, the Egyptians learned how to make full use of the floods by cutting irrigation canals to take the water to land on either side of the river. The "shaduf," a simple water hoist still seen in Egypt today, was used to guide the water into runnels.

The rich Nile mud was very fertile and produced fine crops. Once the waters receded after the floods, most of the people were engaged in plowing and sowing at the same time. At harvest time, the corn was reaped and the flax pulled up; and the crops were carried by donkey to the threshing-floors to be trodden by oxen. The corn was winnowed, then taken to be stored in granaries. Many tomb scenes show these activities.

Below: A scene showing various harvesting activities. The Egyptians expected to harvest twice a year. They grew flax for linen, and wheat and barley for food. They also caught birds and fish, kept chickens and grew produce in their gardens. A proportion of the local produce was paid in taxes to the government. You can see men cutting the corn and carrying it to the threshing area. In the foreground, women winnow the grain.

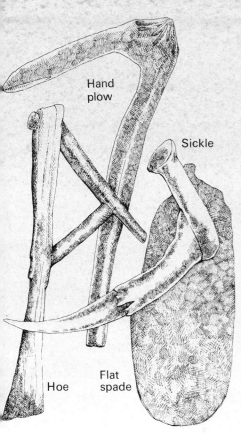

Hand plow

Sickle

Hoe

Flat spade

As well as the tomb scenes, actual tools provide evidence about Egyptian agriculture. The community at Kahun grew its own food, and agricultural tools were found there. Made of wood, some of these designs are still used today in parts of the world. They include hoes, used like picks to break up or scrape the ground; scoops for winnowing; plows; and sickles made of wood with the original flint saws cemented into the sickle to form a cutting edge. There were rakes and shell scoops, as well as whetstones and stone rubbers for grinding the grain.

Examination of the teeth of mummies has revealed that most Egyptian teenagers and adults suffered very badly from attrition (the wearing away of the outer surface of the teeth), which would have caused severe toothache and abscesses. This was because the bread which formed an important part of their diet contained a great deal of grit and sand, and consequently wore away their teeth. Other foods included fruit, vegetables, pulses and, for the wealthy, meat, fish and fowl. Beer and barley wine were also produced, and a variety of sweet cakes made of grain and honey. The diet of most ordinary people, however, consisted of bread, beer and onions.

Politics

The Egyptians aimed to achieve an ordered balance both in their private lives and in their political institutions. This idea, called "Ma'at," was personified by a goddess who symbolized the correct balance of the universe and of Egypt. She was also the goddess of law and lawyers.

Ancient Egypt had a carefully worked out and efficient system of government. As early as the Old Kingdom, the Egyptians were taking a census of the fields every two years, and a census of cattle. There was a universal taxation system, and many officials were employed by the government to administer and collect the taxes. In theory, every Egyptian was also obliged to work for the king on irrigation, building and other projects when required. However, only the poorest people actually did this; the wealthy bought their way out of the obligation. The king and his agents could also requisition or demand the use of animals and ships owned by private people or by the temples, since, in theory, he owned everything in Egypt.

Slavery, where an individual has no legal rights, was unknown, but certain groups of people could be owned, bought and sold by others, and legally set free. Yet even these people could own and dispose of possessions, own land and bequeath it to their children, marry free women, and keep servants. These groups, which included some prisoners of war, were owned by the state, the temples or private individuals.

Above: This Middle Kingdom wooden tomb model represents a procession of bearers bringing offerings. They carry jars and baskets, and two of the women are holding birds in their hands. Such processions would have been seen on all the estates throughout Egypt.

Despite heavy taxation, Egyptians enjoyed at least some private freedom to make fun of the established order. There is a hint of social criticism in these scenes of cats and mice painted on ostraka.

These potsherds used for drawing or writing were discovered in the rubbish heaps of the royal workmen's town, Deir el Medina. Sketched by the same men who decorated the king's tomb, they represent the nobles as mice and the servants as cats. They may illustrate the story of the War of the Cats and the Mice.

The crown needed wealth to provide for the upkeep of the king's household, to make royal gifts to the nobility, to pay (in kind) the wages of the state officials, and to pursue its foreign policy. One of its most important duties was building up reserve stocks of food for the years of famine. The king had command of all foreign trade, and also owned all the quarries and mines.

Within Egypt, taxation provided much of the government's wealth. The various districts paid their taxes in kind. Every year, government experts visited the countryside and measured the land: a list of landholders and tenants was made, and the probable tax yield was assessed. Later, other officials came to fix the amount of tax, then to collect it – using force if necessary. Although the law gave both rich and poor the right to be heard, and protected wives and families, punishments were severe. People found guilty of capital offences would be thrown to the crocodiles, losing not only their life but the chance of a proper burial for their body. Beatings were common for minor offences, and some crimes were punishable by cutting off the offender's ears or nose. In some cases, a whole family would be punished for a crime committed by one of its members.

Right: Amenophis III receives Nubian tribute; in the foreground, the Viceroy of Nubia is rewarded with gold collars, a mark of royal favor. Egypt's gold was obtained from the Eastern Desert and Nubia. It formed a major part of Nubia's regular tribute. Since there was no system of money in Egypt until the later periods, barter (the exchange of goods) was used. Some fixed weights were also introduced, and gold, silver and copper values were given to certain goods. Gold "deben" (a unit of weight), represented as yellow rings in the wall scenes, are often shown, being presented with other items.

Education and Writing

Egyptian hieroglyphs developed from pictures. A system seems to have been fully worked out as early as 3100 BC, when the first known hieroglyphic writings appear. They were used, especially carved on monuments, for more than 3000 years. For business documents, letters and administrative purposes, however, various cursive scripts were developed, which were easier and quicker to use. One of these, known as Hieratic, occurs in the earliest dynasties and was used regularly till about 800 BC. Each character is a simplification of a hieroglyphic sign. Another cursive script, Demotic, was used in documents from the end of the 7th century BC. It became the general form of writing business, legal and literary documents for nearly a thousand years, while hieroglyphs were used on stone inscriptions and Hieratic for religious literature. Although it primarily developed from business Hieratic, Demotic had its own grammar and a new vocabulary.

The final stage of the ancient Egyptian language is to be found in Coptic, a language which continued to be used by the Christian inhabitants of Egypt after the Arab invasion in the 7th century AD. It consisted of the ancient dialects, now written in Greek characters with the addition of some new signs to express Egyptian sounds which did not occur in Greek. Many scholars attempted to decipher hieroglyphs, but it was a Frenchman, Jean-François Champollion, who finally did so, announcing his discovery in 1822. The decipherment was made possible by the finding of the famous Rosetta Stone which is inscribed with the same decree in Greek, Demotic and hieroglyphs.

Above: A painted limestone statue of a scribe, holding a roll of papyrus. Scribes were very important because they could read and write, and formed the bureaucracy of the State. It was an honored profession which brought many benefits. One famous Wisdom Text says, "Behold, there is no calling that is without a master except (that of) a scribe, and he is the master".

Right: Papyrus was the usual writing material used by scribes, although potsherds or flakes of limestone were a cheaper substitute often used by schoolchildren. The papyrus plant was cultivated by the Egyptians to make ropes, baskets, sandals and writing rolls. The pith from the stems, beaten and stuck together, turned into strips which were then rolled up. A thin reed with a frayed tip was used as a brush, though in the 3rd century BC, this was replaced by the stylus – a reed with a fine, sharpened point. Black ink was generally used, but red ink marked certain special features such as the beginning of a new paragraph. Hieroglyphs and Hieratic could be written vertically or horizontally on the papyrus.

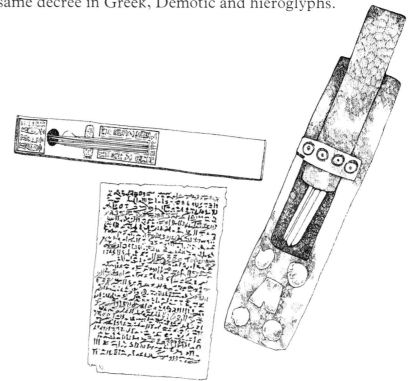

Above: Children were taught in groups. They sat cross-legged on the ground and recited passages in chorus. Great emphasis was put on good manners and courtesy to older people, and dishonesty, idleness, and bad temper were considered bad character faults. "Spend no day in idleness or you will be beaten," children were told, "Do not be lazy, or you will have to be made obedient by correction; do not spend time in day-dreaming or you will surely come to a bad end".

"A boy's ear is on his back – he listens when he is beaten". There is no one account of education in Egypt. Most sons were probably taught a trade by their fathers, and girls learned homecrafts from their mothers. However, there may have been some formal schooling for the poorer classes in village schools. The children of the nobility were taught with the royal children in the palace school, and some higher education was given to future scribes, lawyers and doctors in the temples by the specialist priests. There were also schools to train future officials.

Children learned to read by chanting, and practised writing model letters and exercises, some of which have survived. These exercises were not only intended to train the pupils to write, but were often copies of wise sayings to teach and inspire them. There would also have been some instruction in mathematics, astronomy, astrology and practical arts, and sports and games to train the character. The Egyptians wanted to produce students who not only knew how to read and write, but also fitted well into the society. This is clearly brought out in the "Wisdom Literature" which survives, where advice on how to behave and live correctly in society is given in the form of wise sayings from an older man to his pupil. Teachers used corporal punishment and, as we read in the following passage, lamented bitterly when displeased with their pupils:

"I am told that you neglect your studies and devote yourself entirely to pleasure. You trail from street to street smelling of beer. Beer robs you of all human respect, it affects your mind, and here you are like a broken rudder, good for nothing . . . you have been found performing acrobatics on a wall! Ah, if only you knew that wine was an abomination, if only you would give up liquor and think of something other than tankards of beer!"

Trade and War

The Egyptians needed to obtain silver and additional supplies of wood, copper and certain spices from other lands. Sometimes these could be acquired as booty after military conquests, as tribute or gifts, but frequently they were bought through trade.

Egypt was a country rich in resources, which produced fine crops and had a relatively small population. It could therefore use its surplus goods for trade with other countries, exporting cereals, textiles, paper, dried fish and some luxury items. The main export trade was monopolized by the government. By the New Kingdom (around 1450 BC), royal agents were frequently sent, by land and sea, to obtain wood for building from the Lebanon, metals from Asia, and incense from the land of Punt.

Punt had been known to the Egyptians in the Old Kingdom, but the most detailed accounts of journeys there date from the Middle and New Kingdoms. Its exact location is still uncertain, although it was near the Red Sea, probably in the area of modern Somaliland. Queen Hatshepsut of the 18th Dynasty (1504–1483 BC), who ruled Egypt as a king, built a fine temple to the god Amun at Deir el-Bahri, near Thebes. On its walls is a record, in pictures and inscriptions, of the famous expedition which she sent to Punt. The Egyptians traded by barter with the people of Punt, who apparently received them in a friendly manner, their queen greeting and receiving the Egyptian envoys.

Right: This scene shows men carrying incense trees onto the Egyptian ships visiting the land of Punt. It is on a wall in the Temple of Queen Hatshepsut at Deir el-Bahri, where the queen's famous expedition to Punt is depicted. Incense was regularly used in temple rituals in Egypt, and the Egyptians made frequent visits to Punt where fine incense-bearing trees grew. They either brought back incense in ready-made balls, or the actual incense trees. These were transported in baskets to protect their roots, and replanted in Egypt in the temple gardens. In the temple area at Deir el-Bahri, it is still possible to see the roots of one of these trees.

War

Natural barriers – seas and deserts – protected Egypt from constant invasion, and the rich agriculture provided more than enough food for the population. So the Egyptians had no need to fight wars continuously. They were essentially a peace-loving people. However, it was necessary to protect Egypt's borders, and, from early times, they established supremacy over the Nubians who lived to the south to ensure Egypt had steady gold supplies. Early raiding expeditions were later increased to maintain allegiance to Egypt, and by the Middle Kingdom (c.1900 BC) the kings began to realize the need to colonize Nubia more effectively. They built a string of fortresses with thick brick walls in the region of the Second Cataract and beyond. These housed not only large garrisons but also officials and scribes, and soon became major centers of influence. They were enlarged and developed in the New Kingdom.

In about 1600 BC, Egypt was invaded by the Hyksos and this completely changed the Egyptian attitude to war. Having driven out the Hyksos, the Egyptians of the New Kingdom pursued a more aggressive policy of conquest in Syria and Palestine, and continued to dominate Nubia. Previously, men had been conscripted into the army as the need arose, but now a professional standing army was established. The weapons of the Old and Middle Kingdoms – slings, bows, spears, daggers, maces and axes, and leather or wooden shields – were supplemented by others the Hyksos had introduced: the horse and chariot, the curved sword, and more armor.

The King was commander-in-chief of the army, and led his troops into battle. Most of the soldiers were infantry; chariots existed from the New Kingdom, but there was no cavalry. The navy was an auxiliary branch of the army, carrying troops and supplies. It was not used as a fighting force until the late New Kingdom. Even in the Old Kingdom, foreign mercenaries were recruited. They were increasingly employed,

and are shown wearing their own battle-dress and carrying their own weapons. This scene shows a reconstruction of a fortress in Nubia as Egyptian soldiers march out to subdue the Nubians. Our evidence for this and for what we know about Egyptian warfare generally comes from archaeological excavations, models of soldiers found in tombs, wall scenes and inscriptions in temples, as well as actual weapons.

Glossary

BITUMEN: Mineral pitch or asphalt.

CANOPIC JARS: Jars used to contain the preserved internal organs of the deceased that were removed during mummification.

CARTONNAGE: A term used in Egyptology to describe the material used for some coffins, head-masks and chest- and foot-covers for mummies. It was made of papyrus, mixed with a gummy substance.

CATARACTS: A series of rocky outcrops across the Nile, south of the modern town of Aswan. None of the six cataracts takes the form of a waterfall, but they stop free navigation of the river.

CURSIVE SCRIPTS: Flowing handwriting as seen in the stages of the Egyptian language we know as Demotic and Hieratic. These developed from picture writing.

ELECTRON MICROSCOPE: A microscope that can show up details in a specimen about one thousand times smaller than would be possible in a normal light microscope. These microscopes are particularly useful in the examination of mummified tissue and insect remains found in mummies and coffins.

EMBALMER: A man engaged in the various stages of mummification.

ENDOSCOPY: The science of using an endoscope, an instrument that allows the scientist to see inside a hollow area or organ in the body.

HIEROGLYPHS: Characters in the picture writing of the Egyptians. They were frequently used for sacred or religious texts.

HISTOLOGY: The science which examines the minute structure of animal or vegetable tissues. It involves the preparation of very thin slices of tissues and their examination under a light microscope. The technique is used on mummified tissues to examine tissue structure and to identify disease.

HYKSOS: A group of people who, about 1700 B.C., entered Egypt and established themselves there as kings. They are thought to have included people from Asia Minor and from the nomadic tribes who lived on Egypt's borders. The Egyptians later drove them out northward into Palestine.

MASTABA: A special type of Egyptian tomb with a superstructure (above ground) and a substructure (below ground). The body was placed in the substructure, the tomb goods in the superstructure.

The shape of the superstructure resembled the benches that can often be seen outside houses in Egypt. So the modern Arabic word "mastaba", meaning "bench" is used to describe them.

MATRIX: A base which gives foundation to something placed onto or embedded into it.

MUD-BRICK: Building bricks made of mud and straw and allowed to dry and harden in the sun.

NATRON: The main chemical used in mummification. It was a salt mixture which occurs in natural deposits, with large proportions of sodium carbonate and sodium bicarbonate.

NUBIA: The ancient land to the south of Egypt, roughly equivalent in the modern Sudan. It was from Nubia that the Egyptians acquired hard stone such as granite, and gold. The Egyptian word for gold was "neb", from which they got the name "Numbia."

POTSHERD: A broken piece of pottery, often used to write on.

ROSETTA STONE: An important inscribed stone which was discovered at Rosetta in the Delta of Egypt. The triple inscriptions on this stone enabled the Egyptologists to decipher Egyptian hieroglyphs.

SANCTUARY: Area of an Egyptian temple where the god's statue was kept, and where the priests performed the daily rituals to the god.

SARCOPHAGUS: A large coffin, usually made of stone.

SCRIBE: An official or public writer, a high office in Egypt. Scribes were also teachers.

SEROLOGY: The science of the reactions, preparation and use of serums. It is used in connection with mummy research to determine the blood groups of the mummies.

SHADUF: A water-lifting device. A beam is pivoted at the top of an upright post; at one end of the beam a rope is attached with a bucket. At the other end of the beam is a counterweight. The bucket is lowered by hand into the river, raised and emptied into an irrigation channel, and then lowered back into the water.

WISDOM LITERATURE: A collection of instruction texts, taking the form of addresses by wise men to students. They included advice on good and bad behavior and on how to live in ancient Egyptian society. They were frequently copied by schoolboys as exercises, to instruct them in wisdom and good prose.

Index

Note: page numbers in italics refer to illustrations.